NOW
Is the Time

301 Inspiring Quotes on Living in the Moment

Jim McMullan

STERLING

New York / London
www.sterlingpublishing.com

To Helene, Sky & Tysun: Thanks for keeping me in the NOW.

STERLING and the distinctive Sterling logo are registered trademarks of
Sterling Publishing Co., Inc.

10 9 8 7 6 5 4 3 2 1

Published by Sterling Publishing Co., Inc.
387 Park Avenue South, New York, NY 10016
© 2008 by Jim McMullan
Distributed in Canada by Sterling Publishing
c/o Canadian Manda Group, 165 Dufferin Street
Toronto, Ontario, Canada M6K 3H6
Distributed in the United Kingdom by GMC Distribution Services
Castle Place, 166 High Street, Lewes, East Sussex, England BN7 1XU
Distributed in Australia by Capricorn Link (Australia) Pty. Ltd.
P.O. Box 704, Windsor, NSW 2756, Australia

Printed in China
All rights reserved

Design by Michael Rogalski

Sterling ISBN: 978-1-4027-5324-4

For information about custom editions, special sales, premium and corporate
purchases, please contact Sterling Special Sales Department at 800-805-5489
or specialsales@sterlingpublishing.com.

CONTENTS

INTRODUCTION

What is this thing we call "the now"? It's here at this very moment . . . and it's here again, and then again, and again.

Most of us live in the past or the future, scarcely in the present. But the past is gone—we can't change that. And we certainly shouldn't ruin today by worrying about the future. The art of enjoying life is to experience one moment at a time.

The now awaits us as we learn how to live in the present. The mind, with its constant chatter, attempts to keep us from feeling the freedom and harmony that the now brings when the mind is quiet and still.

Rest assured that right now you are exactly where you are supposed to be. If you think you should be someplace else, doing something else, you are mistaken. Pay attention to the real things in front of you, and let the rest go. All you have is today—give it your full attention and don't let procrastination be the thief of your time. In the words of Benjamin Franklin, "Never leave that till tomorrow which you can do today."

Once you stop procrastinating, you'll find that getting things done becomes a habit. With the dread and reluctance of postponing behind you, projects that originally seemed difficult will actually be completed quickly and effortlessly. Horace offered this wise observation: "He has half the deed done who has made a beginning." Begin, and the momentum will move you forward.

On the following pages, you will find a collection of quotations that I hope will inspire you to live in the present, to stop procrastinating, and to seize the moment. I trust that this little book will inspire you to seek the peace that comes from being in the now and lift you above the ordinary into the realm of joy and bliss.

The *Do It Now!* clock will remind you to stay present minute by minute, second by second . . . always in the now.

—Jim McMullan

Chapter One

A
FRESH
START

You may have a fresh start any moment you choose, for this thing that we call "Failure" is not the falling down, but the staying down.

—Mary Pickford

Live each day as if your life had just begun.

—Johann Wolfgang von Goethe

Though no one can go back and make a brand new start, anyone can start from now and make a brand new ending.

—Carl Bard

The beginning is always today.

—Mary Wollstonecraft Shelley

To die daily, after the manner of St. Paul, ensures the resurrection of a new man, who makes each day the epitome of life.

—William Osler

Yesterday ended last night. Every day is a new beginning. Learn the skill of forgetting. And move on.

—Norman Vincent Peale

A Fresh Start

Each day the world is born anew for him who takes it rightly.

—James Russell Lowell

Always do your best. What you plant now, you will harvest later.

—Og Mandino

When you feel that you have reached the end and that you cannot go one step further, when life seems to be drained of all purpose: what a wonderful opportunity to start all over again, to turn over a new page.

—Eileen Caddy

Finish each day and be done with it. You have done what you could; some blunders and absurdities have crept in; forget them as soon as you can. Tomorrow is a new day; you shall begin it serenely and with too high a spirit to be encumbered with your old nonsense.

—Ralph Waldo Emerson

Light tomorrow with today!

—Elizabeth Barrett Browning

All our yesterdays are summarized in our Now, and all the tomorrows are ours to shape.

—Hal Borland

A Fresh Start

The journey of a thousand leagues begins from beneath your feet.

—Lao Tzu

I live now and only now, and I will do what I want to do this moment and not what I decided was best for me yesterday.

—Hugh Prather

You better live your best and act your best and think your best today, for today is the sure preparation for tomorrow and all the other tomorrows that follow.

—Harriet Martineau

My view is that life unfolds at its own rhythm. You know, I have never lived a life that I thought I could plan out. And I'm just trying to do the best I can every day. I find I have a lot to get done between the time I get up and the time I go to bed.

—Hillary Rodham Clinton

To be seeing the world made new every morning, as if it were the morning of the first day, and then to make the most of it for the individual soul as if each were the last day, is the daily curriculum of the mind's desire.

—John Huston Finley

A Fresh Start

Now this is not the end. It is not even the beginning of the end. But it is, perhaps, the end of the beginning.

—Winston Churchill

As for the Future, your task is not to foresee but to enable it.

—Antoine de Saint-Exupéry

Like as the waves make towards the pebbled shore,
So do our minutes hasten to their end;
Each changing place with that which goes before,
In sequent toil all forwards do contend.

—William Shakespeare

Learn from the past, set vivid, detailed goals for the future, and live in the only moment of time over which you have any control: now.

—Denis Waitley

The man least dependent upon the morrow, that is, the person living in and enjoying the moment, goes to meet the morrow most cheerfully.

—Epicurus

I got the blues thinking of the future, so I left off and made some marmalade. It's amazing how it cheers one up to shred oranges and scrub the floor.

—D. H. Lawrence

A Fresh Start

The future belongs to those who prepare for it today.

—Malcolm X

Today a thousand doors of enterprise are open to you, inviting you to useful work. To live at this time is an inestimable privilege, and a sacred obligation devolves upon you to make right use of your opportunities. Today is the day in which to attempt and achieve something worthwhile.

—Grenville Kleiser

Every day you wake up is a beautiful day.

—John Wayne

Each day is a little life.

—Arthur Schopenhauer

Now is the accepted time, not tomorrow, not some more convenient season.
It is today that our best work can be done and not some future day or future year. It is today that we fit ourselves for the greater usefulness of tomorrow.
Today is the seed time, now are the hours of work, and tomorrow comes the harvest and the playtime.

—W. E. B. Du Bois

Today is the only time we can possibly live.

—Dale Carnegie

A Fresh Start

You cannot run away from a weakness; you must some time fight it out or perish; and if that be so, why not now, and where you stand?

—Robert Louis Stevenson

Don't let yesterday use up too much of today.

—Cherokee Indian proverb

Life is for us today. There will be no change for tomorrow unless we do the changing today.

—Ernest Holmes

Today is yesterday's pupil.

—Benjamin Franklin

He who has lived a day has lived an age.

—Jean de La Bruyère

We live in a moment of history where change is so speeded up that we begin to see the present only when it is already disappearing.

—R. D. Laing

A Fresh Start

Today is a new day. You will get out of it just what you put into it.

—Mary Pickford

You cannot escape the responsibility of tomorrow by evading it today.

—Abraham Lincoln

Yesterday is history, tomorrow is a mystery, and today is a gift; that's why they call it the present.

—Eleanor Roosevelt

If we are ever to enjoy life, now is the time—not tomorrow, nor next year, nor in some future life after we have died. The best preparation for a better life next year is a full, complete, harmonious, joyous life this year. Today should always be our most wonderful day.

—Thomas Dreier

Today is unique. Don't let its wonderful moments go by unnoticed and unused.

—Pat Boone

Each day, each hour, an entire life.

—Juan Ramón Jiménez

A Fresh Start

No matter what looms ahead, if you can eat today, enjoy the sunlight today, mix good cheer with friends today, enjoy it and bless God for it. Do not look back on happiness—or dream of it in the future. You are only sure of today; do not let yourself be cheated out of it.

—Henry Ward Beecher

Happy the man, and happy he alone,
He who can call today his own;
He who, secure within, can say,
Tomorrow, do thy worst, for I have lived today.

—John Dryden

I live a day at a time. Each day I look for a kernel of excitement. In the morning, I say: "What is my exciting thing for today?" Then, I do the day. Don't ask me about tomorrow.

—Barbara Jordan

To those leaning on the sustaining infinite, today is big with blessings.

—Mary Baker Eddy

Today is the day in which to express your noblest qualities of mind and heart, to do at least one worthy thing which you have long postponed.

—Grenville Kleiser

Only the person who lives for today lives at all.

—Joachim du Bellay

Apparently there is nothing that cannot happen today.

—Mark Twain

We should every night call ourselves to an account;
What infirmity have I mastered today? What passions
opposed? What temptation resisted? What virtue
acquired? Our vices will abort of themselves if they
be brought every day to the shrift.

—Seneca

Chapter Two

Appreciating
NOW

And if there is not any such thing as a long time, nor the rest of our lives, nor from now on, but there is only now, why then, now is the thing to praise and I am very happy with it.

—Ernest Hemingway

Learn from yesterday, live for today, hope for tomorrow. The important thing is not to stop questioning.

—Albert Einstein

Hold to the now, the here, through which all future plunges to the past.

—James Joyce

One of the most tragic things I know about human nature is that all of us tend to put off living. We are all dreaming of some magical rose garden over the horizon instead of enjoying the roses that are blooming outside our windows today.

—Dale Carnegie

Yesterday is but a dream, tomorrow but a vision. But today well lived makes every yesterday a dream of happiness, and every tomorrow a vision of hope. Look well, therefore, to this day.

—Sanskrit proverb

Appreciating Now

The present is burdened too much with the past. We have not time, in our earthly existence, to appreciate what is warm with life, and immediately around us.

—Nathaniel Hawthorne

My future starts when I wake up every morning . . . Every day I find something creative to do with my life.

—Miles Davis

If only we knew the real value of a day.

—Joseph Farrell

The secret of health for both mind and body is not to mourn for the past, worry about the future, or anticipate troubles, but to live in the present moment wisely and earnestly.

—Gautama Buddha

Every second is of infinite value.

—Johann Wolfgang von Goethe

Every minute of life carries with it its miraculous value, and its face of eternal youth.

—Albert Camus

Appreciating Now

It is children only who enjoy the present; their elders either live on the memory of the past or the hope of the future.

—Sébastien-Roch Nicolas de Chamfort

For today and its blessings, I owe the world an attitude of gratitude.

—Clarence E. Hodges

Gratitude for the present moment and the fullness of life now is true prosperity.

—Eckhart Tolle

A man should hear a little music, read a little poetry, and see a fine picture every day of his life, in order that worldly cares may not obliterate the sense of the beautiful which God has implanted in the human soul.

—Johann Wolfgang von Goethe

How small a portion of our life it is that we really enjoy! In youth we are looking forward to things that are to come; in old age we are looking backward to things that are gone past; in manhood, although we appear indeed to be more occupied in things that are present, yet even that is too often absorbed in vague determinations to be vastly happy on some future day when we have time.

—Charles Caleb Colton

Appreciating Now

I am real for I am always in the now, in the present. The past is in memory, the future in imagination. You are complete here and now, you need absolutely nothing.

—Sri Nisargadatta Maharaj

Chapter Three

Do
it
NOW

He has half the deed done who has made a beginning.

—Horace

One of these days is none of these days.

—Henry G. Bohn

Now is the operative word. Everything you put in your way is just a method of putting off the hour when you could actually be doing your dream.

—Sam Ewing

What is not started today is never finished tomorrow.

—Johann Wolfgang von Goethe

The biggest sin is sitting on your ass.

—Florynce R. Kennedy

Deal with the difficult while it is yet easy;
Deal with the great while it is yet small.

—Lao Tzu

The wise does at once what the fool does at last.

—Baltasar Gracián

How soon "not now" becomes "never."

—Martin Luther

Yesterday is rarely too early but tomorrow is frequently too late.

—Richard Clarke

When now becomes eventually, then finally
becomes never.

—Brad Schreiber

Don't think, just do.

—Horace

One of these days is just a day of the weak.

—Greg Hickman

There is nothing so fatal to character as half-finished tasks.

—David Lloyd George

Tomorrow is often the busiest day of the week.

—Spanish proverb

We cannot do everything at once, but we can do something at once.

—Calvin Coolidge

The greatest amount of wasted time is the time not getting started.

—Dawson Trotman

Procrastination is opportunity's assassin.

—Victor Kiam

Now is the only time we can ever act.

—Ernest Holmes

The beginning is the most important part of the work.

—Plato

I love deadlines. I like the whooshing sound they make as they fly by.

—Douglas Adams

We shall never have more time. We have, and always had, all the time there is. No object is served in waiting until next week or even until tomorrow. Keep going . . . Concentrate on something useful.

—Arnold Bennett

Procrastination is one of the most common and deadliest of diseases and its toll on success and happiness is heavy.

—Wayne Dyer

IF and WHEN were planted, and NOTHING grew.

—Anonymous

You don't have to see the whole staircase, just take the first step.

—Martin Luther King Jr.

He who hesitates is last.

—Mae West

Procrastination is like a credit card: it's a lot of fun until you get the bill.

—Christopher Parker

The secret of getting ahead is getting started.

—Sally Berger

A year from now you may wish you had started today.

—Karen Lamb

Nothing is so fatiguing as the eternal hanging on of an uncompleted task.

—William James

Every duty which is bidden to wait returns with seven fresh duties at its back.

—Charles Kingsley

Anyone can do any amount of work, provided it isn't the work he is supposed to be doing at that moment.

—Robert Benchley

It is an undoubted truth, that the less one has to do, the less time one finds to do it in.

—Lord Chesterfield

To think too long about doing a thing often becomes its undoing.

—Eva Young

If you want to make an easy job seem mighty hard, just keep putting off doing it.

—Olin Miller

What may be done at any time will be done at no time.

—Scottish proverb

There's nothing to match curling up with a good book when there's a repair job to be done around the house.

—Joe Ryan

Don't wait. The time will never be just right.

—Napoleon Hill

The chief cause of failure and unhappiness is trading what we want most for what we want at the moment.

—Anonymous

He that is good for making excuses is seldom good for anything else.

—Benjamin Franklin

After all is said and done, there is usually more said than done.

—Anonymous

The poison of lateness pushes away all greatness.

—Laura Teresa Marquez

The really happy people are those who have broken the chains of procrastination, those who find satisfaction in doing the job at hand. They're full of eagerness, zest, productivity. You can be, too.

—Norman Vincent Peale

The old saying that "success breeds success" has something to it. It's that feeling of confidence that can banish negativity and procrastination and get you going the right way.

—Donald Trump

Putting off an easy thing makes it hard, and putting off a hard one makes it impossible.

—George H. Lorimer

Chapter Four

Happiness
NOW

My creed is that: Happiness is the only good. The place to be happy is here. The time to be happy is now. The way to be happy is to make others so.

—Robert Green Ingersoll

We know nothing of tomorrow; our business is to be good and happy today.

—Sydney Smith

A day is a span of time no one is wealthy enough to waste.

—Anonymous

Learn to enjoy every minute of your life. Be happy now. Don't wait for something outside of yourself to make you happy in the future. Think how really precious is the time you have to spend, whether it's at work or with your family. Every minute should be enjoyed and savored.

—Earl Nightingale

I, not events, have the power to make me happy or unhappy today. I can choose which it shall be. Yesterday is dead, tomorrow hasn't arrived yet. I have just one day, today, and I'm going to be happy in it.

—Groucho Marx

Happiness Now

One of the keys to happiness is a bad memory.

—Rita Mae Brown

The foolish man seeks happiness in the distance, the wise grows it under his feet.

—James Oppenheim

Having spent the better part of my life trying either to relive the past or experience the future before it arrives, I have come to believe that in between these two extremes is peace.

—Anonymous

Realize that true happiness lies within you. Waste no time and effort searching for peace and contentment and joy in the world outside.

—Og Mandino

Derive happiness in oneself from a good day's work, from illuminating the fog that surrounds us.

—Henri Matisse

Be content with what you have; rejoice in the way things are. When you realize there is nothing lacking, the whole world belongs to you.

—Lao Tzu

Happiness cannot be traveled to, owned, earned, worn or consumed. Happiness is the spiritual experience of living every minute with love, grace and gratitude.

—Denis Waitley

Many people think that if they were only in some other place, or had some other job, they would be happy. Well, that is doubtful. So get as much happiness out of what you are doing as you can and don't put off being happy until some future date.

—Dale Carnegie

NOTES

Happiness is like manna; it is to be gathered in grains, and enjoyed every day.

—Tyron Edwards

I try to learn from the past, but I plan for the future by focusing exclusively on the present. That's were the fun is.

—Donald Trump

Remember that happiness is a way of travel—not a destination.

—Roy M. Goodman

Happiness Now

Dip into your own treasure, for the truth you seek is closer to you than you are to yourself. There is nothing to seek! There is no space in which things are separate from each other, and there is no time when something not yet, or no longer, is. Everything is simultaneous. Everything is here and now.

—Wolfgang Kopp

The true felicity of life is to be free from anxieties and perturbations; to understand and do our duties to God and man, and to enjoy the present without any serious dependence on the future.

—Seneca

Chapter Five

Here
and
NOW

Everything that ever happened is still happening. Past, present and future keep happening in the eternity which is Here and Now.

—James Broughton

I never think of the future. It comes soon enough.

—Albert Einstein

All things are complete in us now.

—Mencius

Everything is present here and now. What good would gaining an inch of land do you when you're already standing smack-dab in the middle of it? Where would you seek? The ancient Chinese said: "If you seek the Tao, then look beneath the soles of your feet."

—Wolfgang Kopp

Flowers flower here and now, birds sing here and now. If we could only turn off the mind with its thoughts, ideas, concepts and dramas, we would contact this amazing reservoir of nowness.

—Harry Kovair

Here and Now

God made the world round so we would never be able to see too far down the road.

—Isak Dinesen

If it be now, 'tis not to come; if it be not to come, it will be now; if it be not now, yet it will come: the readiness is all.

—William Shakespeare

If not me, who? And if not now, when?

—Mikhail Gorbachev

For it is here—in the now—where we find our True
Self, which lies behind our physical body, shifting
emotions, and chattering mind.

—Russell E. DiCarlo

Eternity is not something that begins after you are
dead. It is going on all the time. We are in it now.

—Charlotte Perkins Gilman

Now is eternity; now is the immortal life. Here this
moment, by this tumulus, on earth, now; I exist in it.

—Richard Jefferies

There is never time in the future in which we will work out our salvation. The challenge is in the moment; the time is always now.

—James Baldwin

An everlasting now reigns in nature, which hangs the same roses on our bushes which charmed the Roman and the Chaldean in their hanging gardens.

—Ralph Waldo Emerson

Now is the time for all good men to come to.

—Helen Keller

Let us not look back in anger, nor forward in fear, but around in awareness.

—James Thurber

The future is a deceitful time that always says to us, "Not yet," and thus denies us. The future is not the time of love: what man truly wants he wants now. Whoever builds a house for future happiness builds a prison for the present.

—Octavio Paz

Never anticipate tomorrow's sorrow; live always in this paradisal now.

—Omar Khayyám

Immortality will come to such as are fit for it; and he who would be a great soul in the future must be a great soul now.

—Ralph Waldo Emerson

Because everything is here and now, where and what do you seek? Now is here and here is now. If you want to experience the reality of your being, you must thoroughly immerse yourself in the now. How else can you experience here except now? How can you experience now when you are caught up in tomorrow or the day after tomorrow, when your thoughts are scattered here and there?

—Wolfgang Kopp

Rejoice in the things that are present; all else is beyond thee.

—Michel de Montaigne

Happiness is a butterfly, which, when pursued, is always just beyond your grasp, but which, if you will sit down quietly, may alight upon you.

—Nathaniel Hawthorne

If you worry about what might be, and wonder what might have been, you will ignore what is.

—Anonymous

You are there now. What was never lost
can never be found.
Nothing is there to come, and nothing past,
but an eternal now does always last.

—Abraham Cowley

What alone is ours, the living now.

—William Wordsworth

It is difficult to live in the present, ridiculous to live in the
future, and impossible to live in the past. Nothing is as far
away as one minute ago.

—Jim Bishop

Touch a button and hear, at every level of your life, the iron doors shutting out the past—the dead yesterdays. Touch another and shut off, with a metal curtain, the future—the unborn tomorrows. Then you are safe—safe for today! The load of tomorrow, added to that of yesterday, carried today, makes the strongest falter. Waste of energy, mental distress, nervous worries dog the steps of a man who is anxious about the future.

—William Osler

The Truth is that the only power there is, is contained within this moment: It is the power of your presence. Once you know that, you also realize that you are responsible for your inner space now—nobody else is—and that the past cannot prevail against the power of the now.

—Eckhart Tolle

Here and Now

You must live in the present, launch yourself on every wave, find your eternity in each moment.

—Henry David Thoreau

I live for the present always. I accept this risk. I don't deny the past, but it's a page to turn.

—Juliette Binoche

A preoccupation with the future not only prevents us from seeing the present as it is but often prompts us to rearrange the past.

—Eric Hoffer

What you need to know about the past is that no matter what has happened, it has all worked together to bring you to this very moment. And this is the moment you can choose to make everything new. Right now.

—Anonymous

It's being here now that's important. There's no past and there's no future. Time is a very misleading thing. All there is ever, is the now. We can gain experience from the past, but we can't relive it; and we can hope for the future, but we don't know if there is one.

—George Harrison

Here and Now

Rash indeed is he who reckons on the morrow, or haply on days beyond it; for tomorrow is not, until today is past.

—Sophocles

Something beyond! The immortal morning stands
 Above the night, clear shines her prescient brow;
  The pendulous star in her transfigured hands
   Lights up the now.

—Mary Clemmer Ames

Chapter Six

Letting
Go of the
Past

Living the past is a dull and lonely business; looking back strains the neck muscles, causing you to bump into people not going your way.

—Edna Ferber

With the past, I have nothing to do; nor with the future, I live now, and will verify all past history in my own moments.

—Ralph Waldo Emerson

If you are still talking about what you did yesterday, you haven't done much today.

—Anonymous

No matter the bad things that happened in past time, let's try to live the best we can now.

—Ziggy Marley

Past and future veil God from our sight; burn up both of them with fire.

—Rumi

Losers live in the past. Winners learn from the past and enjoy working in the present toward the future.

—Denis Waitley

Letting Go of the Past

Die to the past every moment. You don't need it. Only refer to it when it is absolutely relevant to the present. Feel the power of this moment and the fullness of being. Feel your presence.

—Eckhart Tolle

Today was once the future from which you expected so much in the past.

—Anonymous

One problem with gazing too frequently into the past is that we may turn around to find the future has run out on us.

—Michael Cibenko

Never agonize over the past or worry over the future. Live this day and live it well.

—Peace Pilgrim

You can clutch the past so tightly to your chest that it leaves your arms too full to embrace the present.

—Jan Glidewell

What happened in the past that was painful has a great deal to do with what we are today, but revisiting this painful past can contribute little or nothing to what we need to do now.

—William Glasser

Letting Go of the Past

Trust no Future, howe'er pleasant!
Let the dead Past bury its dead!
Act,—act in the living Present
Heart within, and God o'erhead!

—Henry Wadsworth Longfellow

The more anger towards the past you carry in
your heart, the less capable you are of loving in
the present.

—Barbara DeAngelis

The past is a guidepost, not a hitching post.

—L. Thomas Holdcroft

There is no distance on this earth as far away as yesterday.

—Robert Nathan

Live your life each day, as you would climb a mountain. An occasional glance towards the summit keeps the goal in mind, but many beautiful scenes are to be observed from each new vantage point.

—Harold B. Melchart

Do not lose yourselves in the past, do not run after the future. The past no longer is, the future has not yet come.

—Gautama Buddha

Letting Go of the Past

The past is the textbook of tyrants. Those who are solely governed by the past stand like Lot's wife, crystallized in the act of looking backward, and forever incapable of looking before.

—Herman Melville

Tomorrow's a fantasy and yesterday's gone . . . there's only today.

—Helene Slack

He who spends time regretting the past loses the present and risks the future.

—Francisco de Quevedo

Reflect on your present blessings, of which every man has many; not on your past misfortunes, of which all men have some.

—Charles Dickens

We should not fret for what is past, nor should we be anxious about the future; men of discernment deal only with the present moment.

—Chanakya

Fear not for the future, weep not for the past.

—Percy Bysshe Shelley

It's but little good you'll do a-watering the last year's crop.

—George Eliot

I have made it a rule of my life never to regret and never to look back. Regret is an appalling waste of energy . . . you can't build on it; it's only good for wallowing in.

—Katherine Mansfield

Chapter Seven

The Time Is NOW

Now is the constant syllable ticking from the clock of time.

—M. F. Tupper

The time is now, the place is here. Stay in the present. You can do nothing to change the past, and the future will never come exactly as you plan or hope for.

—Dan Millman

Time is what keeps the light from reaching us. There is no greater obstacle to God than time.

—Meister Eckhart

There is only one time that is important—now! It is the most important time because it is the only time that we have any power.

—Leo Tolstoy

You will never find time for anything. If you want time you must make it.

—Charles Buxton

The butterfly counts not months but moments, and has time enough.

—Rabindranath Tagore

I wasted time, and now doth time waste me.

—William Shakespeare

Now is the only time. How we relate to it creates the future. In other words, if we're going to be more cheerful in the future, it's because of our aspiration and exertion to be cheerful in the present. What we do accumulates; the future is the result of what we do right now.

—Pema Chödrö

As if you could kill time without injuring eternity.

—Henry David Thoreau

One may walk over the highest mountain one step at a time.

—John Wanamaker

Overcoming fear and worry can be accomplished by living a day at a time or even a moment at a time. Your worries will be cut down to nothing.

—Robert Anthony

The best thing about the future is that it only comes one day at a time.

—Abraham Lincoln

The Time Is Now

Always hold fast to the present hour.

—Johann Wolfgang von Goethe

He who thinks to reach God by running away from the world, when and where does he expect to meet him? . . . We are reaching him here in this very spot, now at this very moment.

—Rabindranath Tagore

Life consists not in holding good cards but in playing those you hold well.

—Josh Billings

No thought, no action, no movement, total stillness; now.

—Henry Suso

The good old days are now.

—Tom Clancy

People are always asking about the good old days. I say, why don't you say the good now days?

—Robert M. Young

We seem to be going through a period of nostalgia, and everyone seems to think yesterday was better than today. I don't think it was, and I would advise you not to wait ten years before admitting today was great. If you're hung up on nostalgia, pretend today is yesterday and just go out and have one hell of a time.

—Art Buchwald

Life is now . . . this day, this hour . . . and is probably the only experience of the kind one is to have.

—Charles Macomb Flandrau

'Tis but a short journey across the isthmus of now.

—Christian Nestell Bovee

The Present, the Present is all thou hast
 For thy sure possessing;
  Like the patriarch's angel hold it fast
   Till it gives its blessing.

—John Greenleaf Whittier

Life, we learn too late, is in the living, in the tissue of every day and hour.

—Stephen Leacock

The old days were the old days. And they were great days. But now is now.

—Don Rickles

The Time Is Now

Write it on your heart that every day is the best day
of the year.

—Ralph Waldo Emerson

The intellect has little to do on the road to discovery.
There comes a leap in consciousness, call it intuition
or what you will, and the solution comes to you and
you don't know how or why.

—Albert Einstein

The future is now.

—Nam June Paik

Don't be fooled by the calendar. There are only as many days in the year as you make use of. One man gets only a week's value out of a year while another man gets a full year's value out of a week.

—Charles Richards

It is only possible to live happily ever after on a day-to-day basis.

—Margaret Bonnano

Expecting is the greatest impediment to living. In anticipation of tomorrow, it loses today.

—Seneca

The best things in life are nearest: Breath in your nostrils, light in your eyes, flowers at your feet, duties at your hand, the path of right just before you. Then do not grasp at the stars, but do life's plain, common work as it comes, certain that daily duties and daily bread are the sweetest things in life.

—Robert Louis Stevenson

Today is today and tomorrow we may be down the drain of eternity.

—Euripides

Chapter Eight

seize the
DAY

Seize the day, put no trust in tomorrow.

—Horace

The right man is the one that seizes the moment.

—Johann Wolfgang von Goethe

Now or never.

—Aristophanes

Lose not yourself in a far off time, seize the moment that is thine.

—Johann Cristoph Friedrich von Schiller

Go for it now. The future is promised to no one.

—Wayne Dyer

History is more or less bunk. It's tradition. We don't want tradition. We want to live in the present and the only history that is worth a tinker's damn is the history we make today.

—Henry Ford

Seize the Day

As you go the way of life, you will see a great chasm. Jump. It is not as wide as you think.

—Joseph Campbell

Leap, and the net will appear.

—Julia Cameron

Courage doesn't always roar. Sometimes courage is the quiet voice at the end of the day saying, "I will try again tomorrow."

—Mary Anne Radmacher-Hershey

Today is life—the only life you are sure of. Make the most of today. Get interested in something. Shake yourself awake. Develop a hobby. Let the winds of enthusiasm sweep through you. Live today with gusto.

—Dale Carnegie

I will act now. Success will not wait. If I delay, success will become wed to another and lost to me forever. This is the time. This is the place. I am the person.

—Og Mandino

Seize the Day

To yackety–yak about the past is for me, time lost. Every morning I wake up saying, "I'm still alive—a miracle." And so I keep pushing.

—Jacques Cousteau

Let him who would enjoy a good future waste none of his present.

—Roger Babson

The dogmas of the quiet past are inadequate to the stormy present. The occasion is piled high with difficulty, and we must rise with the occasion. As our case is new, so we must think anew and act anew.

—Abraham Lincoln

Start by doing what's necessary; then do what's
possible; and suddenly you are doing the impossible.

—Saint Francis of Assisi

Gather ye rose-buds while ye may,
Old Time is still a-flying;
And this same flower that smiles today,
Tomorrow will be dying.

—Robert Herrick

Lose no time; be always employed in something useful.

—Benjamin Franklin

Seize the Day

Twenty years from now, you will be more disappointed by the things you didn't do, than by the ones you did. So throw off the bowlines. Sail away from the safe harbor. Catch the trade winds in your sails. Explore. Dream.

—Mark Twain

Whatever you can do, or dream you can, begin it. Boldness has genius, power, and magic in it.

—Johann Wolfgang von Goethe

It is never too late to be what you might have been.

—George Eliot

Life is very short and what we have to do must be done in the now.

—Audre Lorde

Living is a form of not being sure, not knowing what next or how. The moment you know how, you begin to die a little. The artist never entirely knows. We guess. We may be wrong, but we take leap after leap in the dark.

—Agnes de Mille

Do it! I say. Whatever you want to do, do it now! There are only so many tomorrows.

—Michael Landon

Seize the Day

We cannot escape fear. We can only transform it into a companion that accompanies us on all our exciting adventures . . . Take a risk a day—one small or bold stroke that will make you feel great once you have done it.

—Susan Jeffers

Look not mournfully into the past. It comes not back again. Wisely improve the present. It is thine. Go forth to meet the shadowy future, without fear.

—Henry Wadsworth Longfellow

I take responsibility for myself and what I do now.

—Paul Gascoigne

The innovation point is the pivotal moment when talented and motivated people seek the opportunity to act on their ideas and dreams.

—W. Arthur Porter

I believe there is something doing somewhere, for every man ready to do it. I believe I'm ready, right now.

—Elbert Hubbard

The distance is nothing; it's only the first step that is difficult.

—Marie de Vichy-Chamrond, marquise du Deffand

Seize the Day

In any moment of decision, the best thing you can do is the right thing, the next best thing is the wrong thing, and the worst thing you can do is nothing.

—Theodore Roosevelt

Don't wait for someone to take you under their wing. Find a good wing and climb up underneath it.

—Frank C. Bucaro

Chapter Nine

This
PRESENT
Moment

What at this moment is lacking?

—Rinzai

We hurry through the so-called boring things in order to attend to that which we deem more important, interesting. Perhaps the final freedom will be a recognition that every thing in every moment is essential and that nothing at all is important.

—Helen M. Luke

The passing moment is all we can be sure of; it is only common sense to extract its utmost value from it.

—W. Somerset Maugham

How wonderful it is that nobody need wait a single moment before starting to improve the world.

—Anne Frank

Life can be found only in the present moment. The past is gone, the future is not yet here, and if we do not go back to ourselves in the present moment, we cannot be in touch with life.

—Thich Nhat Hanh

Use your precious moments to live life fully every single second of every single day.

—Marcia Wieder

Life is made of millions of moments, but we live only one of these moments at a time. As we begin to change this moment, we begin to change our lives.

—Trinidad Hunt

Only when your consciousness is totally focused on the moment you are in can you receive whatever gift, lesson, or delight that moment has to offer.

—Barbara DeAngelis

I always say to myself, what is the most important thing we can think about at this extraordinary moment.

—François de La Rochefoucauld

Be fully in the moment, open yourself to the powerful energies dancing around you.

—Ernest Hemingway

I have the happiness of the passing moment, and what more can mortal ask?

—George Robert Gissing

This—this was what made life: a moment of quiet, the water falling in the fountain, the girl's voice . . . a moment of captured beauty. He who is truly wise will never permit such moments to escape.

—Louis L'Amour

Realize that now, in this moment of time, you are creating. You are creating your next moment. That is what's real.

—Sara Paddison

The living moment is everything.

—D. H. Lawrence

Love the moment. Flowers grow out of dark moments. Therefore, each moment is vital. It affects the whole. Life is a succession of such moments and to live each one is to succeed.

—Corita Kent

Shakespeare says, we are creatures that look before and after; the more surprising that we do not look around a little, and see what is passing under our very eyes.

—Thomas Carlyle

We must not allow the clock and the calendar to blind us to the fact that each moment of life is a miracle and mystery.

—H. G. Wells

Who makes quick use of the moment is a genius of prudence.

—Johann Kaspar Lavater

This Present Moment

A man of wisdom lives in the now. He knows that this moment is all there is. Yesterday was and tomorrow will come.

—Harry Kovair

Let anyone try, I will not say to arrest, but to notice or to attend to, the present moment of time. One of the most baffling experiences occurs. Where is it, this present? It has melted in our grasp, fled ere we could touch it, gone in the instant of becoming.

—William James

If you surrender completely to the moments as they pass, you live more richly those moments.

—Anne Morrow Lindbergh

Take my advice: Immerse yourselves exclusively in the now. Free yourselves of everything! Be now at this moment truly here—without thoughts, without concepts, and without impressions.

—Wolfgang Kopp

You are, at this moment, standing, right in the middle of your own "acres of diamonds."

—Earl Nightingale

I can feel guilty about the past, apprehensive about the future, but only in the present can I act. The ability to be in the present moment is a major component of mental wellness.

—Abraham Maslow

The future is made of the same stuff as the present.

—Simone Weil

Right now what is lacking? I am here, you are there, the trees are happy, the sky is beautiful, what is lacking? How can there be more perfection than there is right this moment? Everything is perfect as it is.

—Bhagwan Shree Rajneesh

Nothing ever gets anywhere. The earth keeps turning round and gets nowhere. The moment is the only thing that counts.

—Jean Cocteau

Life is simply a series of such moments to be experienced one right after another. If you attend to the moment you are in and stay connected to your soul and remain happy, you will find that your heart is filled with positive feelings.

—Sydney Banks

Each moment, whatsoever you are doing, do it totally. Simple things—taking a bath; take it totally, forget the whole world; sitting, sit; walking, walk, above all don't wobble; sit under the shower and let the whole existence fall on you. Be merged with those beautiful drops of water falling on you. Small things: cleaning the house, preparing food, washing clothes, going for a morning walk—do them totally—be totally present.

—Bhagwan Shree Rajneesh

It is in your moments of decision that your destiny
is shaped.

—Anthony Robbins

Write down the thoughts of the moment. Those that
come unsought for are commonly the most valuable.

—Francis Bacon

As we look deeply within, we understand our perfect
balance. There is no fear of the cycle of birth, life and
death. For when you stand in the present moment,
you are timeless.

—Rodney Yee

No time like the present.

—Mary de la Rivière Manley

I don't think of the past. The only thing that matters is the everlasting present.

—W. Somerset Maugham

I scarcely remember counting upon happiness. I look not for it if it be not in the present hour. Nothing startles me beyond the moment. The setting sun will always set me to rights or if a sparrow come before my window I will take part in its existence and pick about the gravel.

—John Keats

The water you touch in a river is the last of what has passed, and the first of what is coming. Thus, it is with present time.

—Leonardo da Vinci

I am in the present. I cannot know what tomorrow will bring forth. I can know only what the truth is for me today. That is what I am called upon to serve, and I serve it in all lucidity.

—Igor Stravinsky

Those who talk about the future are scoundrels. It is the present that matters.

—Louis-Ferdinand Céline

The present is the ever moving shadow that divides yesterday from tomorrow. In that lies hope.

—Frank Lloyd Wright

The Present is the living sum-total of the whole Past.

—Thomas Carlyle

Abridge your hopes in proportion to the shortness of the span of human life; for while we converse, the hours, as if envious of our pleasure, fly away: enjoy, therefore, the present time, and trust not too much to what tomorrow may produce.

—Horace

This Present Moment

We may make our future by the best use of the present. There is no moment like the present.

—Maria Edgeworth

Real generosity toward the future lies in giving all to the present.

—Albert Camus

Take all reasonable advantage of that which the present may offer you. It is the only time which is ours. Yesterday is buried forever, and tomorrow we may never see.

—Victor Hugo

Every situation, every moment—is of infinite worth;
for it is the representative of a whole eternity.

—Johann Wolfgang von Goethe

Let us attend to the present, and as to the future we shall
know how to manage when the occasion arrives.

—Pierre Corneille

What is really momentous and all important with
us is the present, by which the future is shaped
and colored.

—John Greenleaf Whittier

Learning to live in the present moment is part of the path of joy.

—Sarah Ban Breathnach

My past is my wisdom to use today . . . my future is my wisdom yet to experience. Be in the present because that is where life resides.

—Gene Oliver

Look upon every day as the whole of life, not merely as a section; and enjoy and improve the present without wishing, through haste, to rush on to another.

—Jean Paul Richter

INDEX

(127)

ACKNOWLEDGMENTS

A big thanks to Carlo DeVito at Sterling Innovation for seeing the magic and saying yes to my idea—and to my always patient and perceptive editor Joelle Herr, who kept me in the moment. Another big thanks to Michael Rogalski for his excellent design. A special hug to my agent, Sheree Bykofsky, who was there to guide and advise me. I thank my son Sky for holding the idea in mind all these years, and my friends Brad Schreiber, Tom Dunsmuir, Jon Nordheimer, and Bill Noble for their encouragement and wisdom.

And a special thank you to Baba Ram Dass and Eckhart Tolle for showing me how to stay tuned into the NOW.

ABOUT THE AUTHOR

Jim McMullan has had seven books published, including *Actors As Artists*, *Musicians As Artists*, *Instant Zen*, and *Happily Ever After*. Now retired after a forty-year film and television career, Jim and his wife Helene live, sail, and meditate on the New Jersey shore.